ESCAPING THE ILLUSION OF HAPPINESS

A Guide to Overcome Struggles and Embrace Living

Olivia Tranquil

WHY THIS BOOK?

Unique Perspective on Happiness: Unlike many self-help books that focus solely on achieving happiness as a constant state, this book challenges readers to rethink their understanding of happiness, revealing the traps of societal expectations and self-imposed pressures.

Practical, Actionable Strategies: The book is filled with practical exercises, mindfulness practices, and actionable strategies designed to help readers identify and overcome their struggles. It's not just about theory; it's about making real changes in your life.

Comprehensive Approach to Well-being: By addressing mindfulness, vulnerability, letting go of control, resilience, relationships, purpose, and passion, the book offers a holistic approach to well-being that goes beyond superficial happiness to foster deep, lasting fulfillment.

Accessibility for All Readers: Whether you're a self-help enthusiast or someone skeptical of the genre, the book's straightforward, jargon-free language makes the concepts accessible and relatable to a broad audience.

Personal Growth Journey: This book acts as a guide for a personal growth journey, encouraging self-reflection and self-discovery. It's not just a one-time read but a resource to come back to as you continue to grow and evolve.

Evidence-Based Insights: Drawing on psychological research, mindfulness practices, and real-life stories of transformation, the book offers credible, evidence-based insights into the nature of happiness and personal transformation.

Empowerment to Face Life's Challenges: Readers will feel empowered to face their struggles head-on, armed with the knowledge and tools to navigate life's challenges and embrace living fully and authentically.

Building Meaningful Relationships: By exploring the role of relationships in our happiness and struggles, the book guides how to cultivate deeper connections with others, enriching one's life and the lives of those around them.

Discovering and Pursuing Passions: The book encourages readers to find and follow their passions and purposes, providing a path to a more meaningful and satisfying life beyond the conventional pursuit of happiness.

Continuous Support and Inspiration: The book is designed to be a source of continuous support and inspiration, with each chapter offering new insights and tools to help readers navigate their journey toward a life of fulfillment.

"Escaping the Illusion of Happiness" is more than just a book; it's a companion for anyone looking to break free from the happiness trap and embark on a fulfilling journey toward living a meaningful life.

FOR WHOM IS THIS BOOK INTENDED?

Self-Help Seekers: Individuals actively searching for guidance on personal development, mental health improvement, and strategies for dealing with life's challenges. They are likely consumers of self-help literature, workshops, and seminars.

Mindfulness and Wellness Enthusiasts: People interested in mindfulness, meditation, and holistic approaches to well-being. This group values practices that promote mental, emotional, and spiritual health.

Young Professionals: Those in their 20s and 30s facing the pressures of career building, societal expectations, and personal fulfillment. They are looking for ways to balance professional ambitions with personal happiness.

Midlife Individuals: Persons experiencing a midlife crisis or seeking meaning and purpose in the middle stages of life. They might be questioning their life choices and looking for a path to genuine satisfaction.

Those Experiencing Life Transitions: Individuals going through significant life changes, such as career shifts, relationship changes, or losing a loved one. This group seeks support and guidance for navigating these transitions with resilience and positivity.

Mental Health Advocates and Professionals: Therapists, counselors, and coaches looking for resources to recommend to clients or to enhance their understanding of happiness and fulfillment.

Parents and Educators: Adults responsible for guiding others, seeking to impart wisdom on living a balanced and fulfilling life. They are interested in learning for themselves and teaching the younger generation about true happiness beyond material success.

Recovery Groups: People in recovery from addiction or overcoming other personal challenges, looking for inspiration and practical tools to rebuild their lives and find joy in the process.

Readers of Philosophy and Psychology: Those interested in the theoretical aspects of happiness, well-being, and human psychology. This audience appreciates books that offer depth, backed by research and philosophical insight.

TABLE OF CONTENTS

[ix]

INTRODUCTION

In a cozy attic filled with the light of a setting sun, Maya found herself lost in her painting. Surrounded by artworks that showed her quest for happiness, she hoped each brushstroke would bring her closer to joy. Yet, despite her talent and the applause she received, true happiness seemed just out of reach. Each painting, though beautiful, left her feeling empty inside.

Then, one day, everything changed. Maya discovered a book that made her realize she had been chasing happiness in the wrong way. This book, "Escaping the Illusion of Happiness," opened her eyes to the truth that her search for happiness through perfection and others' approval was why she felt so unfulfilled.

This realization hit Maya hard, but it also gave her a new perspective. She began to see her art not as a means to gain happiness but as a way to express her true self. Freed from the need to make every painting perfect, Maya started to experiment with her art. She let her emotions guide her brush, creating pieces that were bold, raw, and genuine.

As Maya embraced this new approach, the world's reaction to her art changed. Her work no longer sought the admiration of galleries, but it started touching people's hearts. Viewers saw their hopes, fears, and dreams reflected in Maya's art. The connection was deeper than any award or recognition could offer.

Through her journey, Maya learned an invaluable lesson: happiness is not a prize at the end of a chase. It's found in the process of living authentically, accepting imperfections, and expressing oneself truthfully. Her story is not just about art; it's a guide for anyone looking to escape the happiness trap and find joy in being true to themselves.

This book is for those who, like Maya, are searching for genuine happiness. It's a reminder that sometimes, to find what we're looking for, we need to stop the chase and start living. Join us on this journey of self-discovery and learn to embrace your true path to happiness.

CHAPTER 1

UNDERSTANDING HAPPINESS

"Happiness is not something ready-made. It comes from your actions." – Dalai Lama

This profound statement invites us to embark on a journey of self-discovery and understanding, particularly about happiness, a concept as universally sought after as it is misunderstood. As we delve into this exploration, it's crucial to unravel the intricate layers of happiness, distinguish between its transient forms and its true essence, and recognize the societal constructs that often mislead us.

Introduction to the Concept of Happiness

Happiness, at its core, is an elusive state of well-being and contentment, often accompanied by a sense of fulfillment and joy. However, its true nature is complex, subjective, and multifaceted. Across cultures and individuals, the definition of happiness varies significantly, influenced by personal experiences, cultural norms, and even genetic predispositions. This diversity in understanding leads to a rich tapestry of approaches toward achieving happiness, from seeking external pleasures and achievements to cultivating inner peace and gratitude.

Yet, despite its varied interpretations, happiness is the universal currency of the human experience, the ultimate goal that everyone aspires to in their unique ways. It is the driving force behind our actions, decisions, and pursuits, shaping our lives and guiding our paths.

Common Misconceptions and the Societal Happiness Trap

One of the most pervasive misconceptions about happiness is the belief that it is a constant state of euphoria or pleasure that can be achieved and maintained indefinitely. This belief is further fueled by societal norms and media portrayals that equate happiness with material success, physical attractiveness, and perpetual positivity. However, this pursuit of a flawless, uninterrupted state of happiness is not only unrealistic but also detrimental to our well-being.

The societal happiness trap lies in the relentless chase for external validations and accomplishments under the guise of achieving happiness. We are often led to believe that happiness is a linear journey, where acquiring certain milestones—be it wealth, career success, or relationships—will result in everlasting happiness. This illusion distracts us from the true essence of happiness, which is inherently fluid and transient, and places undue pressure on individuals, leading to feelings of inadequacy, disappointment, and even despair when the promised happiness remains elusive.

The Contrast between Fleeting Pleasure and True Happiness

Distinguishing between fleeting pleasures and true happiness is essential in our quest for lasting well-being. Fleeting pleasures, such as the thrill of a new purchase, the excitement of a compliment, or the rush of an adventure, are temporary and external. They provide short-lived boosts of joy but are susceptible to the law of diminishing returns, where each subsequent experience brings less satisfaction, and the pursuit of these pleasures can become an endless, unfulfilling cycle.

True happiness, on the other hand, is characterized by a deep sense of satisfaction, purpose, and joy that is not dependent on external circumstances. It arises from meaningful connections, personal growth, the pursuit of passions, and the ability to embrace life's ups and downs with resilience and gratitude. True happiness is sustainable and enriches our lives, providing a foundation of contentment that can support us through challenges and enhance our experiences of joy.

Exploring the nuanced nature of happiness requires us to peel back the layers of our perceptions and expectations, challenging the societal norms that have long dictated our understanding of what it means to be truly happy. As we embark on this deeper exploration, we'll delve into the intricacies of happiness, debunk myths, and pave the way for a more authentic and fulfilling pursuit of well-being.

Peeling Back the Layers of Happiness

Happiness is not a monolith but a complex mosaic of experiences, emotions, and states of being. At its core, happiness encompasses a range of positive emotions, from the intense joy of a celebratory moment to the serene contentment of a quiet, reflective afternoon. However, the pursuit of happiness is often misconstrued as a relentless chase for continuous positive emotions, sidelining the significance of more subdued, reflective, and even challenging experiences that contribute to a rich and fulfilling life.

To truly understand happiness, we must acknowledge its dual nature. Positive psychology, a field dedicated to the study of what makes life worth living, suggests that experiencing a broad spectrum of emotions, including those less comfortable, is essential for psychological growth and well-being. These emotions, when navigated thoughtfully, can lead to greater resilience, empathy, and a deeper appreciation for the joyful moments when they do occur.

Challenging Societal Norms

Societal norms often present happiness as a destination achieved by following a prescribed set of criteria—success, wealth, beauty, and perpetual youth. This narrow view overlooks the richness of the human experience and the true essence of happiness that comes from within. By challenging these norms, we open ourselves to a broader understanding of happiness that values personal growth, resilience, meaningful relationships, and the pursuit of passions and values that resonate with our deepest selves.

Breaking free from the happiness trap set by societal expectations involves a conscious effort to redefine success and fulfillment on our terms. It means valuing our intrinsic worth over external validations and recognizing that happiness is not the absence of problems but the ability to deal with them effectively and with grace.

Cultivating a Life Rich in Meaning and Genuine Contentment

Shifting our focus from chasing fleeting pleasures to cultivating a life rich in meaning involves several key shifts in perspective and behavior:

Embrace Authenticity: Live in alignment with your true self, values, and passions. Authenticity acts as a compass guiding us toward actions and choices that bring genuine fulfillment.

Cultivate Gratitude: Regularly acknowledging and appreciating what we have, rather than fixating on what we lack, can transform our perspective on happiness and increase our overall sense of well-being.

Build Resilience: Developing resilience helps us to navigate life's inevitable ups and downs with strength and grace, finding growth and meaning in challenges.

Foster Connections: Deep, meaningful relationships are foundational to happiness. Investing time and energy into building and maintaining these connections enriches our lives and supports our well-being.

Pursue Growth and Learning: Happiness is often found in the journey of personal growth and the pursuit of knowledge and skills that challenge and fulfill us.

Live Mindfully: Practicing mindfulness encourages us to live in the present moment, enhancing our experiences of joy and providing clarity in our pursuit of happiness.

By understanding the complex nature of happiness and rejecting the simplistic, externally focused pursuit of pleasure, we can begin to cultivate a life of deep, lasting contentment. This journey is not about denying the negative or striving for an unattainable ideal but about embracing the full spectrum of human experience with openness, resilience, and authenticity.

Self-Reflection Questions for Personal Knowledge

1. What does happiness mean to you? Take a moment to reflect on your definition of happiness. How does it compare to the societal view of happiness? Identify aspects of your definition that may have been influenced by external factors.

____

____

____

____

____

2. Can you recall a moment of intense joy that was not tied to
    an external achievement or validation? Think about a time
    when you felt genuinely happy for no specific reason. What
    were you doing, and what does this tell you about the
    sources of your happiness?

____

____

____

____

____

3. How do societal expectations affect your pursuit of
    happiness? Consider how societal norms and expectations
    have shaped your goals and pursuits. Are there aspects of
    your life where you feel pressured to seek happiness in a
    certain way?

———————————————————

———————————————————

———————————————————

———————————————————

———————————————————

4. What are some simple pleasures or moments of contentment in your life that you might have overlooked? Reflect on the everyday moments that bring you a sense of peace or joy. How can you make more moments like this?

———————————————————

———————————————————

———————————————————

———————————————————

———————————————————

5. How can you incorporate more authentic sources of happiness into your life? Based on your reflections and understanding of true happiness, identify one or two changes you can make to pursue a more genuine form of happiness.

Chapter Summary

In this chapter, "Understanding Happiness," we embarked on a journey to unravel the complex and multifaceted nature of happiness. We began by challenging the common misconceptions and societal norms that often lead us into the happiness trap—a relentless pursuit of happiness defined by external achievements and validations. Through deeper exploration, we distinguished between fleeting pleasures and true happiness, emphasizing that genuine contentment arises from living authentically, embracing a spectrum of emotions, and finding meaning and fulfillment within ourselves.

We dissected the societal pressures that skew our perception of happiness and learned how to redefine happiness on our terms, focusing on internal growth, resilience, meaningful connections, and living in alignment with our true selves. This chapter aimed to shift the reader's focus from seeking ephemeral joys to cultivating

[10]

a life enriched with purpose, authenticity, and a deep sense of well-being.

By challenging our preconceived notions of happiness and embracing a more nuanced understanding, we pave the way for a more fulfilling and authentic pursuit of happiness. The self-reflection questions provided are designed to encourage personal introspection and guide readers toward a deeper, more personal exploration of what happiness truly means to them, laying the foundation for the transformative journey that lies ahead in the subsequent chapters.

CHAPTER 2

THE ROOTS OF UNHAPPINESS

"In the quest for happiness, we must first understand the darkness." – Anon

This chapter delves into the intricate web of factors that sow the seeds of unhappiness in our lives. By understanding these roots, we can start to untangle ourselves from the grip of dissatisfaction and pave our way toward a more fulfilling existence. Unhappiness, much like happiness, is a complex phenomenon influenced by a myriad of factors. Here, we explore some of the most common sources of unhappiness, the profound impact of expectations, comparisons, and societal pressures, and bring these concepts to life through personal stories and case studies.

Identifying Common Sources of Unhappiness

Unhappiness often stems from a disconnect between our desires and our realities. Yet, the sources of this discord are varied and multifaceted. Common culprits include a lack of purpose or meaning in one's life, unfulfilled desires, chronic stress or overwork, poor health or pain, strained relationships, and financial instability. Each of these factors alone can lead to feelings of unhappiness, but when combined or experienced in succession, they can significantly compound the intensity of these feelings.

Another less obvious but equally impactful source of unhappiness is the internal conflict and self-doubt we experience when our actions and lives do not align with our values and beliefs. This dissonance can lead to a profound sense of dissatisfaction and unrest, as we struggle to reconcile our ideals with our lived experiences.

The Role of Expectations, Comparisons, and Societal Pressures

Expectations play a pivotal role in shaping our happiness. Unrealistic expectations, whether self-imposed or instilled by others, can set us up for disappointment and discontent. The expectation to always be happy, successful, and in control can lead to feelings of inadequacy and failure when life inevitably falls short of these ideals.

Comparisons further exacerbate this issue. In today's digital age, where curated lives are constantly showcased on social media, it's easy to fall into the trap of comparing our behind-the-scenes with everyone else's highlight reel. This comparison can skew our perception of our own lives, leading to dissatisfaction and a constant feeling of lacking.

Societal pressures add another layer of complexity. Society often dictates a blueprint for success and happiness, emphasizing milestones like career advancement, marriage, and homeownership as markers of achievement. The pressure to conform to these societal norms can lead to a pursuit of goals that do not align with personal values or desires, resulting in a hollow sense of unhappiness.

Personal Stories and Case Studies

To illustrate these concepts, let's consider the story of Alex, a high-achieving professional who climbed the corporate ladder at a breakneck pace. On paper, Alex's life was the epitome of success: a lucrative job, a luxurious home, and a seemingly perfect family. However, beneath the surface, Alex was profoundly unhappy. The relentless pursuit of success had come at the cost of personal health, relationships, and a sense of purpose. Alex's story highlights the peril of chasing externally defined success without regard to one's well-being and values.

Another case is that of Samira, who constantly compared her life to her peers on social media, leading to a deep sense of inadequacy and unhappiness. Samira's journey of turning off social media notifications and focusing on her personal growth illustrates the power of disconnecting from comparisons and recentering on what truly matters.

Through these stories and others, we see the multifaceted nature of unhappiness and the common threads that weave through many of our experiences. By recognizing and understanding these roots, we can begin to address them, making informed changes toward a happier and more authentic life.

Self-Reflection Questions for Personal Knowledge

1. Reflect on your expectations for yourself and your life. Are they truly your own, or have they been influenced by others—family, friends, society? How do these expectations align with your genuine desires and values?

____

____

____

____

____

2. Reflect on the last time you compared yourself to someone else. How did it make you feel? Consider the aspects of your life you were comparing. Are these comparisons helping you grow, or are they diminishing your sense of self-worth?

____

____

____

____

____

3. Identify a societal pressure you feel strongly about. How has this pressure shaped the choices you've made in your life? Do these choices reflect who you truly are and what you genuinely want, or are they concessions to societal expectations?

____

____

____

____

____

4. Recall a recent moment of unhappiness. Can you trace it back to an unmet expectation, a comparison, or a societal pressure? How might understanding the source of this unhappiness help you address it more effectively?

____

____

____

____

____

5. Consider your values and beliefs. Is there a part of your life where you feel you're not living in alignment with these? How does this misalignment contribute to your unhappiness, and what steps can you take to reconcile this disparity?

Chapter Summary

In Chapter 2, "The Roots of Unhappiness," we explored the complex landscape of factors contributing to unhappiness. The chapter opened with an investigation into common sources of unhappiness, including unmet desires, chronic stress, poor health, strained relationships, and financial instability. We delved into the pivotal role of expectations, comparisons, and societal pressures, illustrating how these factors can set us up for disappointment and discontent by creating unrealistic standards for our lives.

The exploration continued with personal stories and case studies, such as Alex's realization that external success does not equate to internal happiness and Samira's journey towards self-acceptance by stepping away from social media comparisons. These narratives provided concrete examples of how the roots of unhappiness manifest in real life and offered insights into navigating these challenges.

This chapter aimed to illuminate the underlying causes of unhappiness, encouraging readers to reflect on how expectations, comparisons, and societal pressures have shaped their own experiences. By understanding these roots, we can begin to disentangle ourselves from the web of dissatisfaction and move towards a life aligned with our true desires and values. The self-reflection questions were designed to facilitate personal introspection, helping readers identify and address the specific sources of unhappiness in their lives. Through this process, we lay the groundwork for overcoming these challenges and paving a path toward a more fulfilling and authentic existence.

CHAPTER 3

THE PSYCHOLOGY OF STRUGGLE

"Struggle is a never-ending process. Freedom is never really won, you earn it and win it in every generation." – Coretta Scott King

This powerful quote sets the stage for our exploration into the psychology of struggle, a universal aspect of the human condition. Struggle is often perceived as a negative experience, yet it holds the potential for profound personal growth and transformation. In this chapter, we delve into the psychological underpinnings of why we struggle, examine the impact of negative thought patterns and behaviors on our well-being, and provide strategies for recognizing and interrupting these patterns to foster resilience and positive change.

Exploring the Psychology Behind Why We Struggle

At the heart of human struggle lies the conflict between our desires and the reality of our circumstances. This conflict is rooted in our basic psychological needs for autonomy, competence, and relatedness, as outlined by Self-Determination Theory. When these needs are unmet or thwarted, we experience struggle. Additionally, our evolutionary predisposition towards a negativity bias—where we're more attuned to potential threats and failures than to positive outcomes—exacerbates this sense of struggle. This bias helped our ancestors survive but in our modern context often leads to an overemphasis on negative experiences and outcomes.

Our struggles are also influenced by cognitive distortions, such as black-and-white thinking, overgeneralization, and catastrophizing, which can warp our perception of reality and heighten our sense of distress. These mental habits are deeply ingrained in our psyche, often originating from early life experiences and societal conditioning, and they play a significant role in perpetuating our struggles.

The Impact of Negative Thought Patterns and Behaviors on Our Well-Being

Negative thought patterns and behaviors, such as rumination, self-criticism, and avoidance, significantly impact our mental, emotional, and physical well-being. They can trap us in a cycle of stress and despair, diminishing our capacity to see situations clearly and respond to challenges effectively. Chronic engagement in these patterns can lead to mental health issues like anxiety and depression, and even affect our physical health by contributing to a host of stress-related conditions.

Moreover, these negative patterns can sabotage our efforts to achieve goals, maintain healthy relationships, and pursue meaningful change in our lives. They narrow our focus, limit our perceived options, and hinder our ability to problem-solve and adapt, keeping us stuck in a state of perpetual struggle.

Strategies for Recognizing and Interrupting These Patterns

Interrupting negative thought patterns and behaviors requires conscious effort and practice. Let's go into the strategies for recognizing and interrupting negative thought patterns and behaviors, as understanding and applying these techniques can be transformative in overcoming struggles and enhancing overall well-being.

Developing Awareness Through Mindfulness and Reflection

Mindfulness is the practice of paying attention to the present moment, intentionally and without judgment. By cultivating mindfulness, we can become more aware of our thoughts, emotions, and bodily sensations as they arise, observing them without getting caught up in their narrative. This heightened awareness allows us to recognize when we're slipping into negative thought patterns or engaging in harmful behaviors. Mindfulness can be practiced through meditation, mindful walking, or simply by pausing throughout the day to check in with ourselves.

Reflective practices involve taking time to look back on our experiences, thoughts, and feelings, to gain insights into our behaviors and reactions. Journaling is a powerful reflective practice, offering a space to express and explore our inner world, identify patterns of negativity, and contemplate alternative, more constructive responses.

Challenging and Reframing Distorted Thoughts with Cognitive-Behavioral Strategies

Cognitive-behavioral strategies are based on the premise that our thoughts, feelings, and behaviors are interconnected and that changing one can influence others. These strategies involve identifying cognitive distortions—unhelpful ways of thinking that distort reality—and challenging them to adopt a more balanced perspective.

For instance, when engaging in black-and-white thinking (viewing situations in extreme, either-or categories), we can ask ourselves: "Is there a more nuanced way to look at this situation?" Identifying the "shades of gray" helps us realize that life is rarely as binary as our distorted thinking suggests.

Catastrophizing, or imagining the worst possible outcome, can be countered by asking, "What are the odds of this happening, and what are other possible outcomes?" This helps reduce anxiousness and fosters a more realistic overview of situations.

Behavioral Activation to Counteract Inertia

Behavioral activation is a strategy to overcome the inertia that negative thoughts and moods can produce. It involves committing to activities that are aligned with personal values and goals, even when motivation is low. The action of engaging in these activities can, paradoxically, generate the motivation and positive feelings that were initially lacking. This approach is particularly effective for breaking the cycle of depression and anxiety, where withdrawal and avoidance only serve to deepen negative feelings.

Building Resilience with Self-Compassion and Positive Self-Talk

Self-compassion involves treating oneself with kindness, understanding, and support during times of failure or difficulty, rather than harsh self-criticism. Practicing self-compassion can be as simple as asking, "What would I say to a friend in this situation?" and then directing those compassionate responses towards oneself.

Positive self-talk is another resilience-building tool. It involves consciously shifting internal dialogue from negative to positive, encouraging, and supportive messages. This doesn't mean ignoring reality or difficulties but rather approaching them with a mindset that promotes resilience and the belief in one's ability to cope and recover.

Seeking Support from Others

Finally, seeking support plays a crucial role in overcoming struggles. Connecting with others—whether through therapy, support groups, or meaningful relationships—provides a sense of belonging, validation, and perspective that can be incredibly supportive. Sharing our struggles with trusted individuals allows us to feel understood and supported, offering new insights and strategies for coping that we might not have considered on our own.

By understanding and applying these strategies, individuals can significantly impact their ability to recognize and interrupt negative thought patterns and behaviors, paving the way for a life characterized by resilience, growth, and well-being.

Self-Reflection Questions for Personal Knowledge

1. What negative thought patterns do you notice most frequently in your life? Reflect on the specific types of cognitive distortions (like catastrophizing, black-and-white thinking, or overgeneralization) that you tend to fall into. How do they shape your perception of situations?

____

____

____

____

____

2. When you experience a strong emotional reaction, can you identify the underlying thoughts driving that emotion? Consider a recent situation where your emotions felt

overwhelming. Try to trace back to the thoughts that sparked these emotions.

____

____

____

____

____

3. How does your inner critic speak to you, and what does it say? Pay attention to the tone and content of your self-talk, especially during moments of stress or failure. What would a more compassionate response sound like?

____

____

____

____

____

4. Can you recall a time when mindful awareness helped you navigate a difficult moment? If not, imagine how being fully present and non-judgmental could change your response to challenges.

____

____

____

____

____

5. What's one small step you can take to engage in an activity
   that aligns with your values, even if you don't feel like it
   right now? Consider how taking action, regardless of your
   mood, might help shift your perspective or mood.

Chapter Summary

In Chapter 3, "The Psychology of Struggle," we embarked on an exploration into the psychological dynamics underpinning our struggles. Understanding that struggle is an inherent part of the human experience, we delved into the reasons behind why we struggle, emphasizing the roles of unmet psychological needs, our evolutionary predisposition towards a negativity bias, and the impact of cognitive distortions.

We highlighted the significant effects of negative thought patterns and behaviors, such as rumination and avoidance, on our well-being, illustrating how they can perpetuate cycles of stress and diminish our capacity for resilience. By recognizing these patterns, we can begin to interrupt and transform them.

The chapter provided strategies for breaking free from the grip of negative thinking, including developing mindfulness and reflective practices to enhance self-awareness, employing cognitive-behavioral techniques to challenge distorted thoughts, and embracing behavioral activation to overcome inertia. We also discussed the importance of building resilience through self-compassion and positive self-talk and the value of seeking support from others.

This chapter serves as a guide for recognizing and interrupting the negative thought patterns and behaviors that contribute to our struggles. By applying these strategies, readers are empowered to navigate their struggles with greater resilience and to pave the way for a more fulfilling and well-balanced life.

CHAPTER 4

MINDFULNESS AND ACCEPTANCE

"Mindfulness is a way of befriending ourselves and our experience." – Jon Kabat-Zinn

Amid life's tumultuous seas, mindfulness and acceptance serve as anchors, grounding us in the present and allowing us to navigate our struggles with grace and resilience. This chapter delves into mindfulness as a transformative tool for fostering awareness and acceptance, elucidating how these practices can lead to a significant decrease in our struggles. Through practical exercises, we will explore how to integrate mindfulness into our daily lives, enhancing our capacity for joy, resilience, and a deep, fulfilling engagement with life.

Introduction to Mindfulness as a Tool for Awareness and Acceptance

Mindfulness, the art of paying attention to the present moment with openness, curiosity, and a willingness to be with what is, offers a powerful antidote to the challenges and struggles we face. It is not merely a practice but a way of being, one that allows us to observe our thoughts, feelings, and sensations without judgment or resistance. This heightened awareness fosters a profound acceptance of our current experience, liberating us from the futile struggle against reality.

The practice of mindfulness has its roots in ancient traditions, yet its relevance has never been more pronounced than in our modern, fast-paced world. Research in psychology and neuroscience supports its benefits, showing that mindfulness can reduce stress, enhance emotional regulation, and improve overall well-being. By cultivating mindfulness, we learn to detach from the narratives and judgments that often lead to suffering, embracing instead a stance of openness and acceptance towards our experience.

How Acceptance Can Lead to a Decrease in Struggling

Acceptance, in the context of mindfulness, does not imply passivity or resignation but rather an acknowledgment of things as they are. It is the recognition that while we may not have control over every aspect of our lives, we can always choose how we respond.

Acceptance liberates us from the exhausting endeavor of denial and resistance, allowing us to confront reality with clarity and wisdom.

The paradox of acceptance is that by embracing our struggles, we often find that their hold over us diminishes. This doesn't mean our problems disappear, but our relationship to them changes. We no longer identify as closely with our pain or let our challenges define us. Instead, we observe them with compassion and detachment, which opens up space for healing and transformation. Acceptance is thus a crucial step towards decreasing unnecessary suffering and enhancing our ability to cope with life's inherent difficulties.

Transformative Exercises to Cultivate Mindfulness in Daily Life

Cultivating mindfulness does not require special equipment or vast amounts of time; it can be woven into the fabric of our daily lives through simple practices. Here are some exercises to begin integrating mindfulness into your routine:

Mindful Breathing: Take a few minutes each day to pay attention to your breath. Notice the sensation of air entering and leaving your nostrils, the rise and fall of your chest, and the rhythm of your breathing. Whenever your mind wanders, carefully bring back your attention to your breath.

Mindful Eating: Choose one meal or snack each day to eat mindfully. Pay attention to the colors, textures, and flavors of your food. Notice the sensations of chewing and swallowing. Eating mindfully can transform a routine activity into a profound practice of awareness.

Body Scan Meditation: Lie down in a comfortable position and slowly direct your attention through different parts of your body. Notice any sensations, tension, or discomfort without judgment, simply observing what is present.

Mindful Walking: Turn a regular walk into a mindfulness practice by focusing on the sensation of your feet touching the ground, the rhythm of your steps, and the experience of movement. Observe the sights, sounds, and smells around you with fresh eyes and ears.

Mindful Listening: Engage in conversations to pay attention fully and attentively. Notice the tendency to plan your response while the other person is speaking and instead focus on truly hearing their words and understanding their perspective.

By embracing mindfulness and acceptance, we not only navigate our struggles with greater ease but also open ourselves to the richness and depth of our experience.

As we deepen our exploration of mindfulness and acceptance, we come to understand that these practices are not mere techniques but pathways to a profound transformation of our relationship with life's challenges. This transformation is rooted in the shift from a reactive stance, where struggles are met with resistance and aversion, to a responsive stance, characterized by openness and curiosity. Let's continue by exploring how to further integrate mindfulness into our lives, moving beyond exercises into a more sustained mindfulness practice.

Integrating Mindfulness into Everyday Moments

Mindful Communication: Beyond listening, mindful communication involves speaking with intention, clarity, and kindness. Before speaking, take a moment to consider the purpose of your words. Are they true, necessary, and beneficial? This practice fosters more meaningful and compassionate interactions.

Mindfulness in Work and Tasks: Apply mindfulness to your work or daily tasks by fully engaging with the activity at hand. Whether you're working on a project or washing dishes, give it your full attention. Notice the details of your actions and the sensations involved, treating each task as an opportunity to practice presence.

Mindful Response to Stress: When faced with stress or difficulty, pause before reacting. Take a few mindful breaths to ground yourself in the present. This pause creates space for a choice in how you respond, allowing you to act from a place of calm and wisdom rather than being hijacked by immediate emotions.

Expanding Acceptance Beyond the Self

Acceptance of Others: Mindfulness and acceptance can profoundly impact our relationships. By practicing acceptance of others as they are, without trying to change them, we cultivate deeper connections and understanding. This does not mean condoning harmful behavior but rather recognizing the humanity in everyone, including their struggles and imperfections.

Acceptance of Life's Uncertainties: Much of our struggle stems from a desire for certainty and control. Mindfulness teaches us to embrace the inherent uncertainty of life, finding peace in the reality that not everything is within our control. This acceptance can free us from the anxiety of trying to predict and plan every aspect of our lives.

Sustaining Your Practice

Regular Meditation Practice: While the exercises mentioned are powerful, sustaining a regular meditation practice can deepen and solidify the benefits of mindfulness. Dedicate a regular time each day for seated meditation, using guided meditations if helpful.

Mindfulness Retreats and Community: Consider attending mindfulness retreats or joining a mindfulness community. These can provide immersive experiences and a sense of support and shared purpose that enriches your practice.

Continuous Learning: The journey of mindfulness and acceptance is ongoing. Engage with books, courses, and teachings on mindfulness to keep your practice vibrant and evolving.

Embracing Mindfulness as a Way of Life

Ultimately, mindfulness and acceptance become not just practices but a way of life. This shift in perspective changes how we experience every moment, turning ordinary experiences into opportunities for awareness, growth, and connection. By cultivating mindfulness and embracing acceptance, we learn to navigate life's challenges with grace and appreciate the profound beauty of our existence.

This chapter has offered a map for this journey, providing practical exercises and insights to guide your path. As you integrate mindfulness and acceptance into your life, you may discover a deeper sense of peace, resilience, and joy than you thought possible. Remember, the journey is as important as the destination, and each moment is an opportunity to practice, learn, and grow.

Self-Reflection Questions for Personal Knowledge

1. How do you typically react when you encounter stress or discomfort? Reflect on your immediate responses and consider how mindfulness might alter these reactions. Can you identify a recent situation where pausing and observing your feelings could have led to a different outcome?

____

____

____

____

____

2. When was the last time you engaged in an activity fully, without distraction? Think about how it felt to be fully present with that experience. How might bringing this level of presence to more aspects of your life impact your overall well-being?

____

____

____

____

____

3. What are your thoughts on acceptance, particularly regarding situations you cannot change? Have you ever experienced relief from letting go of the struggle against what is? Contemplate how acceptance might be applied to a current challenge in your life.

____

____

____

____

____

4. How often do you find yourself listening to respond rather than listening to understand? Reflect on a recent conversation and consider how mindfulness could enhance your communication and relationships.

____

____

____

____

____

5. In what areas of your life do you feel the urge to have control? Consider how this need for control affects your stress levels and happiness. How might embracing uncertainty and practicing acceptance in these areas change your experience?

____

____

____

____

____

Chapter Summary

Chapter 4, "Mindfulness and Acceptance," explores the transformative power of mindfulness as a fundamental tool for cultivating awareness and fostering acceptance in our lives. The chapter begins with an introduction to mindfulness, defining it as the practice of paying attention to the present moment with openness and without judgment. It emphasizes the importance of mindfulness in recognizing and accepting our current experiences, which, in turn, can lead to a significant decrease in the struggles we face.

We delve into the concept of acceptance, highlighting its role in reducing suffering by allowing us to confront reality with clarity and wisdom. Acceptance is portrayed not as passive resignation but as an active recognition of the truth of our situation, leading to freedom and the possibility of change.

Practical exercises for cultivating mindfulness in daily life are introduced, ranging from mindful breathing and eating to integrating mindfulness into communication, work, and responses to stress. These exercises serve as accessible entry points for anyone looking to incorporate mindfulness into their routine, emphasizing that mindfulness can be practiced at any moment of the day.

The chapter also expands on the idea of acceptance beyond personal struggles, encouraging readers to apply acceptance to relationships and life's uncertainties. This broader application of acceptance is presented as a pathway to deeper connections with others and a more peaceful engagement with life's inherent unpredictability.

In summary, this chapter provides a comprehensive guide to understanding and practicing mindfulness and acceptance. Through practical exercises and insightful discussions, it invites readers on a journey towards a more mindful, accepting, and fulfilling life. By integrating these practices into our daily routines, we open ourselves to the profound joy and resilience that come from living fully in the present moment.

CHAPTER 5

REWRITING YOUR NARRATIVE

"The privilege of a lifetime is to become who you truly are." –
C.G. Jung

In this compelling journey of self-discovery and transformation, the stories we tell ourselves about who we are, what we are capable of, and what we deserve, play a crucial role in shaping our reality. Our personal narratives and belief systems, deeply ingrained through years of experiences and external influences, can either propel us forward or hold us back. Chapter 5 delves into the transformative power of rewriting our narratives, offering techniques to challenge limiting beliefs and craft a new, empowering personal story.

The Power of Personal Narratives and Belief Systems

Our narratives are the stories we believe about ourselves and our place in the world. These narratives are constructed from our experiences, cultural background, societal expectations, and the feedback we receive from others. Similarly, our belief systems are the lenses through which we view the world, influencing how we interpret our experiences, how we react to challenges, and the decisions we make.

When our narratives and beliefs are positive and empowering, they can fuel our growth and lead us to pursue our goals with confidence. However, when they are negative or limiting, they can trap us in a cycle of self-doubt, fear, and stagnation. The first step in rewriting our narrative is recognizing that these stories and beliefs are not fixed truths but interpretations of our experiences that we have the power to change.

Techniques for Challenging and Changing Limiting Beliefs

Identify and Acknowledge: Begin by identifying the limiting beliefs that are holding you back. These might include beliefs about your worth, capabilities, or what you deserve in life. Accepting these beliefs is the first move toward change.

Trace the Origins: Understand where these beliefs come from. Often, limiting beliefs are rooted in past experiences, cultural messages, or things we were told by influential people in our lives.

Tracing their origins can help us see them for what they are—external impositions rather than inherent truths.

Challenge and Reframe: Once you've identified and understood the origins of your limiting beliefs, challenge them. Ask yourself if they are truly accurate. Look for evidence that contradicts these beliefs. Reframe these beliefs by creating new, empowering statements that reflect the person you want to become.

Visualization and Affirmation: Use visualization to imagine yourself living according to your new beliefs. Create affirmations that reinforce your new narrative and repeat them daily to solidify these changes in your mindset.

Crafting a New, Empowering Personal Story

Creating a new personal narrative is an act of imagination and will. It involves envisioning the life you want to lead and the person you want to become, then aligning your beliefs and actions with that vision.

Define Your Values: Your new narrative should be rooted in your core values. Identify what truly matters to you and let these values guide the stories you tell yourself about who you are and what you're capable of.

Set Intentions: Instead of setting fixed goals, set intentions that reflect the journey you want to embark on. Intentions are flexible and can adapt as you grow and change, making them powerful tools for shaping your narrative.

Create a Vision Board: A vision board is a visual representation of your new narrative, filled with images, words, and symbols that represent your goals and aspirations. It serves as a constant reminder of the life you're working to create.

Live Your New Story: Begin to live out your new narrative in small ways every day. Act as if your new beliefs are already true. With each action, you reinforce your new narrative, making it a lived reality.

Rewriting your narrative is not a one-time event but a continuous process of growth and self-reflection. As you evolve, so too will your story. By challenging your limiting beliefs and crafting a new, empowering personal story, you unlock the potential to become who you truly are and lead a life of purpose and fulfillment.

As we journey further into the art of rewriting our narratives, it becomes clear that this process is both liberating and empowering. It's a pathway to shedding old skin and embracing the fullness of our potential. Let's explore additional strategies and insights to deepen this transformative work.

Embracing the Role of the Storyteller in Your Life

Understand Your Power: Recognize that you are the author and the protagonist of your own life story. This realization empowers you to take control and actively shape the narrative, rather than feeling like a passive character in a script written by others.

Gather New Experiences: Your narrative is enriched by the breadth of your experiences. Seek out new challenges, relationships, and learning opportunities. Each new experience is a thread in the tapestry of your story, adding depth, color, and texture.

Mindful Language Use: The language we use internally and externally shapes our reality. Be mindful of the words you choose when thinking about your life and describing your experiences. Shift from a language of limitation to one of possibility and affirmation.

Techniques for Deepening Your Narrative Change

Journaling for Growth: Maintain a journal dedicated to your narrative change. Use it to document insights, challenges, and victories along the way. Reflective writing can clarify your thoughts and feelings, revealing patterns and beliefs that need to be rewritten.

Seek Feedback and Inspiration: Share your evolving narrative with trusted friends or mentors. Feedback can provide new perspectives and inspiration. Additionally, immerse yourself in stories of people who have undergone significant transformations. Their journeys can offer valuable lessons and motivation.

Consistency and Patience: Rewriting your narrative is a gradual process that requires consistency and patience. Embrace small steps and celebrate progress, knowing that each action and thought contributes to your overall transformation.

Crafting a New, Empowering Personal Story

Future Scripting: Engage in future scripting, a powerful exercise where you write about your future life as if it has already happened. Describe your achievements, emotions, and the lifestyle you envision in vivid detail. This practice makes your desired future feel more tangible and achievable.

Align Actions with Narrative: Ensure that your daily actions and decisions align with your new narrative. Each congruent action reinforces your new story, gradually making it your lived reality.

Embrace Flexibility in Your Story: While it's essential to have a clear vision, allow your narrative the flexibility to evolve. Be open to new directions and insights that may emerge, understanding that personal growth is not linear.

Living Your New Narrative

The ultimate goal of rewriting your narrative is not just to change how you see yourself but to transform how you live your life. This new narrative becomes the foundation upon which you build your actions, relationships, and decisions. It influences how you meet challenges, celebrate successes, and interact with the world around you.

As you live out your new narrative, remember that you are a work in progress, and so is your story. It will grow and change as you do, reflecting your journey's complexity, beauty, and depth. By embracing the power to rewrite your narrative, you open yourself up to a world of possibilities, where growth is continuous, and the potential for transformation is boundless.

In closing, let this chapter be a reminder of your agency in crafting the life story you desire and deserve. Your narrative is not just a story about you; it is the essence of your lived experience, a testament to your resilience, and a beacon guiding you toward your fullest expression. Through mindful reflection, deliberate action, and a commitment to growth, you can rewrite your narrative into one of empowerment, fulfillment, and profound joy.

Self-Reflection Questions for Personal Knowledge

1. What is one limiting belief you've identified in your narrative? Reflect on how this belief has shaped your decisions and actions. How does it feel to consider letting go of this belief?

____

____

____

____

____

2. Can you recall a moment when you felt truly empowered? Think about the story you were telling yourself at that time. How did your narrative support this feeling of empowerment?

____

____

____

____

____

3. What new experience would add a positive chapter to your life story? Imagine stepping into this experience. How does it align with the new narrative you wish to create?

____

____

____

____

____

4. How does the language you currently use about yourself support or undermine your new narrative? Identify one

change you can make in your self-talk to reinforce your evolving story.

____

____

____

____

5. What does your future script look like one year from now? Visualize in detail. How does living according to your new narrative change your daily life?

____

____

____

____

Chapter Summary

Chapter 5, "Rewriting Your Narrative," embarks on the transformative journey of understanding and reshaping the personal stories we tell ourselves. It begins by acknowledging the profound power our narratives and belief systems hold over our lives, either propelling us toward our fullest potential or keeping us tethered to past limitations. The chapter underscores the importance of recognizing that these narratives are not fixed truths but perceptions shaped by our experiences and the influence of those around us.

We delve into practical techniques for identifying, challenging, and ultimately changing the limiting beliefs that form the basis of our self-imposed narratives. Strategies such as tracing the origins of these beliefs, reframing them through evidence-based challenges, and utilizing visualization and affirmation practices are explored in depth. These tools not only help in dismantling old stories but also in constructing new, empowering narratives that align more closely with our authentic selves and aspirations.

The chapter emphasizes the active role we must take in crafting our new personal stories, suggesting exercises like future scripting, mindful language use, and aligning daily actions with our desired narrative. It calls for consistent effort, patience, and flexibility, recognizing that our personal stories are ever-evolving works in progress that require ongoing attention and nurturing.

In living out this new narrative, we're encouraged to embrace our agency, celebrating each step toward our envisioned future while remaining open to the journey's inherent unpredictability and lessons. The chapter closes with a powerful reminder of the transformative potential that rewriting our narrative holds — not just in altering our self-perception but in fundamentally changing how we engage with the world.

"Rewriting Your Narrative" is not merely a guide to personal transformation; it's an invitation to embark on a lifelong journey of growth, discovery, and fulfillment. By actively engaging in the process of reshaping our stories, we unlock the door to a life of greater purpose, joy, and empowerment.

CHAPTER 6

EMBRACING VULNERABILITY

"Vulnerability is the birthplace of innovation, creativity, and change." – Brené Brown

In a world that often equates vulnerability with weakness, embracing our vulnerability emerges as a radical act of courage. Chapter 6 delves into the paradoxical strength found in vulnerability and openness, challenging the fear of judgment and rejection, and illuminating how shared vulnerability can forge deeper connections with others. Through this exploration, we discover that vulnerability is not just a path to personal growth but a cornerstone of meaningful relationships and community.

The Strength in Vulnerability and Openness

Vulnerability is the willingness to show up and be seen, to share our true selves, including our fears and aspirations, without knowing the outcome. Far from being a weakness, vulnerability is a profound strength that requires immense courage. It is in our most vulnerable moments that we access the depths of our courage, compassion, and connection.

The strength in vulnerability lies in its ability to break down barriers and illuminate our shared humanity. It allows us to be authentic, fostering an environment where innovation and creativity can flourish. Vulnerability is also the gateway to empathy and understanding, as it invites others to see us as we truly are, facilitating deeper, more genuine interactions.

Overcoming the Fear of Judgment and Rejection

One of the most significant barriers to embracing vulnerability is the fear of judgment and rejection. This fear can keep us from expressing our true selves and pursuing our deepest desires. Overcoming this fear begins with self-compassion and the recognition that our worth is not contingent on external validation.

To navigate this fear, we must also reframe our perspective on judgment and rejection. Instead of viewing them as personal failures, we can see them as opportunities for growth and learning. Embracing vulnerability means accepting the possibility of judgment and rejection while still choosing to be open and authentic.

Techniques to overcome this fear include mindfulness practices to stay present and avoid catastrophizing, and cognitive-behavioral strategies to challenge and reframe negative thoughts about ourselves and how others may perceive us.

Building Deeper Connections with Others Through Shared Vulnerability

Shared vulnerability is a powerful tool for building deeper connections. When we openly share our struggles, fears, and hopes with others, we invite them to do the same, creating a space of mutual trust and understanding. This shared vulnerability can lead to stronger, more supportive relationships, both personally and professionally.

To cultivate shared vulnerability, it's essential to create environments where openness is valued and protected. This includes actively listening, expressing empathy, and withholding judgment when others share their vulnerabilities with us. It also involves being selective about whom we choose to be vulnerable with, ensuring that our openness is met with respect and care.

Techniques for Cultivating Vulnerability

Practice Self-awareness: Recognize and acknowledge your feelings and fears. Understanding your vulnerabilities is the first step in embracing them.

Start Small: Begin by sharing small vulnerabilities with trusted friends or family members. Gradual exposure will build your confidence in being open and vulnerable.

Seek Supportive Communities: Engage with groups or communities where vulnerability is encouraged and valued. This could be a therapy group, a hobby club, or an online community dedicated to personal growth.

Reflect on Experiences: After sharing vulnerably, reflect on the experience. Acknowledge your courage, note how it felt, and consider the response it elicited from others.

Model Vulnerability: Be the change you wish to see by modeling vulnerability in your interactions. Your openness can inspire others to be more vulnerable, creating a positive cycle of connection and understanding.

Embracing vulnerability is not a journey to be undertaken lightly, but it is one rich with rewards. As we learn to be vulnerable, we unlock new levels of authenticity, creativity, and connection, transforming our relationships and ourselves in the process.

As we further explore the landscape of vulnerability, we understand that its embrace is not merely an act of personal courage but a fundamental shift in how we engage with the world and ourselves. Let's delve deeper into the transformative implications of embracing vulnerability, extending our discussion to its role in personal growth, leadership, and fostering community.

Vulnerability as a Catalyst for Personal Growth

Embracing Change and Uncertainty: Vulnerability is intrinsically linked to our ability to embrace change and navigate uncertainty. It challenges us to step out of our comfort zones and confront our fears, fostering resilience and adaptability. By accepting vulnerability, we open ourselves to life's full spectrum of experiences, learning to move through the world with a sense of curiosity and openness to growth.

Cultivating Self-Acceptance: The journey into vulnerability requires a deep dive into self-acceptance. It involves acknowledging our imperfections, forgiving ourselves for our mistakes, and appreciating our strengths and weaknesses alike. This process of self-acceptance is liberating, allowing us to live more authentically and freeing us from the exhausting pursuit of perfection.

Vulnerability in Leadership and Community Building

Fostering Authentic Leadership: In the realm of leadership, vulnerability is transformative. Authentic leaders who embrace vulnerability inspire trust, promote open communication, and encourage a culture of innovation. By showing their willingness to take risks, fail, and learn, leaders create an environment where others feel safe to do the same. This vulnerability-based approach to leadership cultivates teams that are more cohesive, creative, and committed.

Creating Connected Communities: Vulnerability has the power to bring people together, creating communities rooted in empathy and mutual support. When individuals share their stories, challenges, and aspirations, they find common ground, breaking down barriers of isolation and misunderstanding. Communities grounded in shared vulnerability are characterized by a deep sense of belonging and collective resilience, offering a space where individuals can find support, understanding, and encouragement.

Strategies for Embracing Vulnerability in Broader Contexts

Mindful Communication: Practice communicating your thoughts, feelings, and needs openly and honestly, while also being receptive to the vulnerabilities shared by others. This mindful exchange fosters deeper understanding and connection.

Lead with Empathy: Whether in a leadership role or as a member of a community, approach interactions with empathy. Recognize that behind every face is a story marked by its struggles and triumphs. Empathy bridges gaps and builds a foundation for meaningful connections.

Normalize Discussions About Failure and Learning: Cultivate spaces—be it at work, home, or social settings—where discussing failures and lessons learned is encouraged. This normalization of vulnerability can transform how we view challenges and growth, moving from a culture of criticism to one of learning and encouragement.

Engage in Collective Reflection: Participate in or facilitate group reflections where members can share their experiences and insights. This collective vulnerability strengthens community bonds and fosters a shared sense of purpose and identity.

Embrace and Promote Diversity: Recognize that vulnerability manifests differently across cultures, genders, and individual experiences. Embracing and promoting diversity within communities and leadership roles enriches the tapestry of shared experiences, offering a wider range of perspectives and solutions.

Moving Forward with Vulnerability

As we close this chapter on embracing vulnerability, we're reminded that the journey is both deeply personal and universally resonant. Vulnerability is not just a personal challenge but a societal one, requiring shifts in how we communicate, lead, and support one another. It asks us to be brave, to lean into discomfort, and to open ourselves to the transformative power of connection.

Embracing vulnerability is an ongoing practice, a choice to be made again and again. It's a path marked by challenges but illuminated by the potential for profound growth and connection. As we move forward, let us carry the lessons of vulnerability with courage, allowing them to guide us toward more authentic, compassionate, and connected lives.

Self-Reflection Questions for Personal Knowledge

1. When was the last time you felt vulnerable, and what was your immediate reaction? Reflect on this moment. Consider how embracing this vulnerability instead of retreating from it could have led to growth or deeper connection.

____

____

____

____

2. What is one area of your life where fear of judgment or rejection holds you back? Think about the steps you could take to confront this fear. How might your life change if you approached this area with openness and vulnerability?

____

____

____

____

3. Can you identify a leader or public figure who embodies vulnerability? What traits or actions of theirs convey strength through vulnerability to you? How can you incorporate these traits into your leadership style or daily interactions?

____

____

____

____

4. Recall a time when someone else's vulnerability led you to feel more connected to them. How did their openness impact your perception of them and your relationship? Does this experience change how you view the act of sharing vulnerabilities?

____

____

____

____

5. How does the culture within your community or workplace treat vulnerability? Is it seen as a strength or a weakness? What steps can you take to foster an environment where vulnerability is valued and encouraged?

———————————————————————————

———————————————————————————

———————————————————————————

———————————————————————————

———————————————————————————

Chapter Summary

Chapter 6, "Embracing Vulnerability," explores the transformative power of vulnerability in personal growth, relationships, leadership, and community building. The chapter opens with the recognition of vulnerability as a strength, challenging the common misconception that it is a weakness. It emphasizes that true courage lies in the willingness to be open and expose our true selves, despite the fear of judgment or rejection.

The discussion then shifts to overcoming the fear of judgment and rejection, highlighting the importance of self-compassion, reframing perspectives on failure, and the liberating power of accepting vulnerability as part of the human experience.

Techniques such as mindfulness, reflective practices, and seeking supportive communities are recommended to navigate these fears.

Building deeper connections through shared vulnerability is presented as a key benefit of embracing vulnerability. The chapter provides strategies for creating spaces where vulnerability is encouraged, such as practicing empathetic listening, fostering open communication, and promoting an environment of mutual respect and understanding.

The narrative progresses to examine vulnerability in leadership and community contexts, proposing that vulnerability can inspire trust, innovation, and a sense of belonging. It suggests that leaders who embrace their vulnerability can foster more cohesive and resilient teams. Similarly, communities that value shared vulnerability create stronger bonds among their members.

Strategies for integrating vulnerability into broader life contexts include engaging in mindful communication, leading with empathy, normalizing discussions about failure, engaging in collective reflection, and embracing diversity. These approaches help to cultivate an environment where vulnerability is seen as a source of strength and connection.

In closing, "Embracing Vulnerability" serves as a guide and an invitation to view vulnerability not as a flaw but as a fundamental aspect of our humanity that, when acknowledged and embraced, can lead to profound personal transformation and deeper, more meaningful connections with others. The chapter underscores the ongoing nature of this journey, encouraging readers to continuously practice vulnerability in pursuit of a more authentic, connected life.

As you read through this book, what are those intriguing thoughts going through your mind? Write about them.

CHAPTER 7

THE JOURNEY TO SELF-COMPASSION

"Self-compassion is simply giving the same kindness to ourselves that we would give to others." – Christopher Germer

In a world that often prioritizes productivity, comparison, and external success, the art of self-compassion becomes a sanctuary for the soul, a necessary practice for nurturing our inner well-being. Chapter 7 unfolds the journey to self-compassion, highlighting its critical role in overcoming struggles, providing practical advice on cultivating self-compassion and self-care, and exploring the transformative power of forgiveness as an integral aspect of self-compassion.

The Importance of Self-Compassion in Overcoming Struggles

Self-compassion is the practice of treating oneself with kindness, understanding, and forgiveness, especially in the face of mistakes, failures, and personal shortcomings. It involves recognizing our shared humanity, and understanding that suffering and imperfection are part of the human experience.

The significance of self-compassion lies in its profound impact on our mental and emotional resilience. Studies have shown that individuals who practice self-compassion are less likely to experience depression, anxiety, and stress. They are better equipped to navigate life's challenges, recover from setbacks, and pursue their goals with confidence and determination. Self-compassion fosters an internal environment of support and understanding, making it easier to confront and overcome struggles.

How to Practice Self-Compassion and Self-Care

Practicing self-compassion involves several key components:

Mindfulness: Begin with mindfulness, the ability to be present with your thoughts and feelings without judgment. Recognize your suffering without over-identifying with it. Mindfulness creates the space needed to respond to our pain with compassion.

Common Humanity vs. Isolation: Acknowledge that suffering is a part of the shared human experience. This understanding helps to combat feelings of isolation during difficult times, reminding us that we are not alone in our struggles.

Kindness to Oneself: Treat yourself with the same kindness and care you would offer a good friend. This can involve speaking to yourself with gentle and encouraging words, recognizing your worth, and affirming your strengths and efforts.

Self-Care Practices

- **Physical Self-Care:** Engage in activities that nurture your body, such as regular exercise, nutritious eating, and adequate rest.
- **Emotional Self-Care:** Allow yourself to feel and express emotions in healthy ways, seeking support when needed.
- **Mental Self-Care:** Dedicate time to activities that stimulate your mind and foster a positive mindset, such as reading, meditating, or practicing gratitude.

The Role of Forgiveness in Self-Compassion

Forgiveness is a cornerstone of self-compassion. It involves releasing resentment or harsh judgments toward oneself for past mistakes or perceived failures. Forgiveness is not about forgetting or excusing our actions but about acknowledging them with understanding and kindness, allowing ourselves to move forward without being burdened by self-directed anger or guilt.

Practicing Forgiveness

Acknowledge and Accept: Recognize the actions or thoughts you wish to forgive. Accept them as part of your past, understanding that they do not define your worth or future.

Empathize with Yourself: Try to understand the circumstances or emotions that led to those actions. Offer yourself empathy, acknowledging that everyone makes mistakes.

Release and Move Forward: Consciously decide to release the burden of self-blame. Set intentions for how you wish to act differently in the future, using your past as a learning experience.

Embracing the Journey

The journey to self-compassion is both a practice and a commitment to oneself. It asks us to turn inward with kindness, recognize our shared humanity, and foster an environment within ourselves that promotes healing, growth, and unconditional self-acceptance. Through self-compassion, we not only heal and empower ourselves but also extend this kindness outward, enriching our relationships and the world around us.

As we continue to navigate the depths of self-compassion, it's essential to recognize that this journey is both personal and universal. Embracing self-compassion is an act of inner rebellion against a culture that often values harsh self-criticism as a motivator for change. Yet, it is in the gentle embrace of our humanity that true transformation begins. Let's delve further into cultivating a compassionate inner dialogue and extending this compassion into our broader life experience.

Cultivating a Compassionate Inner Dialogue

Understanding the Inner Critic: The first step in cultivating a compassionate inner dialogue is to recognize the voice of the inner critic. This voice often echoes old messages we've received from others, societal expectations, or our fears. While its intention might be to protect us from failure or hurt, it often does so by keeping us small and afraid to take risks.

Transforming the Inner Critic into an Inner Ally: Transforming the inner critic involves acknowledging its presence without allowing it to dictate our self-worth or actions. This transformation requires:

- **Awareness:** Notice when the inner critic is speaking. What triggers it? What does it say?
- **Questioning:** Challenge the inner critic's narratives. Are its statements true? Are they helpful?

- **Reframing:** Replace critical or demeaning thoughts with kinder, more supportive messages. If a friend were in your situation, what would you say to them? Use this as a model for speaking to yourself.

Extending Self-Compassion to Life's Challenges

Navigating Failure and Setbacks: View failures and setbacks as opportunities for learning and growth rather than evidence of unworthiness. Approach these experiences with curiosity and kindness, asking, "What can I learn from this?" rather than defaulting to self-blame.

Embracing Imperfection: Let go of the pursuit of perfection, a common source of suffering. Embrace your imperfections as part of being human. Recognize that growth and learning come from our imperfections and that they make our experiences and contributions uniquely ours.

The Ripple Effects of Self-Compassion

Enhanced Relationships: As we become more compassionate with ourselves, our capacity for empathy and compassion towards others expands. This deepened understanding and kindness can transform our relationships, fostering greater intimacy and connection.

Contribution to a More Compassionate World: Individual practices of self-compassion contribute to a collective shift towards a more compassionate society. As more people reject the internalization of harsh criticism and embrace kindness towards themselves, societal norms around success, failure, and self-worth can begin to shift.

Living a Life Anchored in Self-Compassion

Embracing self-compassion is a lifelong journey, one that enriches every aspect of our being. It requires continuous practice and commitment but offers profound rewards: a life lived with more joy, resilience, and peace. It allows us to meet the world with an open heart, ready to experience its beauty and complexity with courage and kindness.

As you move forward on this journey, remember that self-compassion is not a destination but a way of being. It's a choice to be kind to yourself each day, to forgive yourself for your mistakes, and to treat yourself with the same care and understanding you offer to others. This chapter is your invitation to embark on this transformative path, cultivate a compassionate relationship with yourself, and discover the boundless strength and peace that comes from embracing your humanity with kindness.

Self-Reflection Questions for Personal Knowledge

1. How do you react to personal mistakes or failures? Reflect on your immediate internal response when you realize you've made a mistake or failed at something. Do you approach these moments with self-criticism or self-compassion?

____

____

____

____

2. Can you identify a specific situation where your inner critic was particularly loud? Think about what it said and how it made you feel. How could a more compassionate response have altered your experience of that situation?

____

____

____

____

3. What does the concept of 'embracing imperfection' mean to you? Consider areas in your life where you struggle with perfectionism. How might accepting imperfection in these areas free you or improve your well-being?

____

____

____

____

____

4. Recall a time when you extended compassion to someone else. How did it feel to offer that kindness? Now, imagine directing that same compassion toward yourself. What changes when you become the recipient of your compassion?

____

____

____

____

5. What are three compassionate statements you can tell yourself next time you face a setback or challenge? Write them down. How do these statements make you feel compared to your usual self-talk in such situations?

____

____

____

____

____

Chapter Summary

Chapter 7, "The Journey to Self-Compassion," illuminates the transformative power of treating oneself with kindness, understanding, and forgiveness. It begins with an exploration of the importance of self-compassion in overcoming struggles, highlighting how a compassionate approach to self can significantly reduce the impact of stress, anxiety, and depression, thereby fostering resilience and a positive outlook on life.

The chapter delves into practical strategies for practicing self-compassion and self-care, emphasizing mindfulness, recognizing our common humanity, and being kind to ourselves as foundational steps. It offers guidance on transforming the inner critic into an inner ally through awareness, questioning, and reframing negative self-talk into supportive and encouraging dialogue.

Forgiveness is introduced as a crucial component of self-compassion, with the chapter providing insights into how forgiving oneself for past mistakes and perceived shortcomings can lead to healing and personal growth. It outlines steps for practicing forgiveness, including acknowledging and accepting one's actions, empathizing with oneself, and making a conscious decision to release self-blame.

The narrative then expands on the ripple effects of self-compassion, illustrating how this inward kindness can enhance relationships, contribute to more compassionate communities, and inspire a collective shift towards a more empathetic society. The chapter underscores that self-compassion is not only a personal journey but also a societal one, with the potential to cultivate a culture of understanding and kindness.

In conclusion, "The Journey to Self-Compassion" serves as both a guide and an invitation to embrace self-compassion as a way of life. It reassures readers that while the path may require continuous effort and mindfulness, the rewards—increased joy, resilience, and peace—are profound and life-changing. The chapter encourages readers to start treating themselves with the same compassion they readily offer others, thus embarking on a journey of healing, growth, and deep, fulfilling self-acceptance.

CHAPTER 8

CULTIVATING GRATITUDE AND JOY

"Gratitude turns what we have into enough." – Anonymous

This profound statement captures the essence of gratitude—a transformative force that enriches our lives, turning the ordinary into the extraordinary and fostering a deep, abiding sense of joy. In Chapter 8, we embark on a journey to explore the transformative power of gratitude, introduce simple yet profound practices to cultivate gratitude and joy in everyday life and examine the impact of gratitude on our overall happiness and well-being.

The Transformative Power of Gratitude

Gratitude is much more than a fleeting feeling of thankfulness in response to kindness or good fortune; it's a profound state of appreciation that can radically alter our perspective on life. It shifts our focus from what is lacking to what is present, from dissatisfaction to contentment, and from entitlement to humility. This shift in perspective is transformative, allowing us to see the abundance that surrounds us and fostering a deep sense of joy that is not contingent on external circumstances.

Research in positive psychology has consistently shown that practicing gratitude can have a significant impact on our mental and emotional well-being. It reduces stress, enhances mood, and promotes resilience. Grateful individuals tend to be happier, more optimistic, and less prone to anxiety and depression. Furthermore, gratitude strengthens relationships, encourages generosity, and builds a supportive social network, which are essential components of a fulfilling life.

Simple Practices to Cultivate Gratitude and Joy in Everyday Life

Cultivating gratitude is a practice—a deliberate choice to acknowledge and appreciate the goodness in our lives. Here are several practices to help you cultivate gratitude and joy daily:

Keep a Gratitude book: Set aside a few minutes every day to pen down three things you are grateful for. These can be as simple as a warm cup of coffee, a kind word from a friend, or the beauty of a sunset. The act of writing reinforces the feeling of gratitude and makes it more tangible.

Gratitude Meditation: Engage in a daily meditation focused on gratitude. Visualize the things you are grateful for and allow the feeling of appreciation to fill your heart. This practice not only cultivates gratitude but also brings a sense of peace and contentment.

Express Gratitude to Others: Make it a habit to express your appreciation to the people in your life. A simple "thank you," a heartfelt note or a gesture of kindness can deepen connections and spread joy.

Gratitude Reminders: Place visual reminders in your environment to practice gratitude. This could be a sticky note on your mirror, a gratitude stone in your pocket, or a set reminder on your phone. These cues can help bring your attention back to gratitude throughout the day.

Nature Walks: Spend time in nature, and allow yourself to be filled with wonder and appreciation for the beauty around you. Nature's magnificence is a powerful reminder of the abundance we often take for granted.

The essence of Gratitude on Overall Happiness and Well-Being

The practice of gratitude not only enhances our immediate mood but also contributes to a sustained increase in overall happiness and well-being. By focusing on what we have, rather than what we lack, we cultivate a mindset of abundance. This abundance mindset is associated with greater satisfaction with life, higher energy levels, and improved health outcomes.

Gratitude also plays a crucial role in building and maintaining relationships. It fosters a cycle of kindness and generosity, creating a positive social environment that benefits everyone involved. In this way, gratitude not only improves our own lives but also has a ripple effect, enhancing the well-being of our communities.

Embracing Gratitude as a Way of Life

Cultivating gratitude and joy is not a one-time act but a lifestyle—a commitment to viewing the world through the lens of appreciation and wonder. Follow this guide on your journey to integrate gratitude into your daily life, transforming your experience of the world and deepening your connection to yourself and others. By practicing gratitude, we unlock the fullness of life, discovering joy in the ordinary and finding contentment in the here and now.

As we further explore the realms of gratitude and joy, it becomes evident that these practices are not merely exercises in positivity but profound strategies for living a deeply fulfilling life. Let's delve deeper into how integrating gratitude into our daily lives can profoundly impact our well-being, relationships, and perspective on the world.

Expanding the Practice of Gratitude

Gratitude in Difficult Times: One of the most powerful aspects of gratitude is its ability to transform our experience during challenging times. While it may seem counterintuitive to look for things to be grateful for amid hardship, doing so can provide a lifeline, a way of navigating through the darkness with hope and resilience. It's about finding light in the shadows and acknowledging that even in the hardest moments, there are glimmers of beauty and kindness.

Cultivating a Gratitude Mindset: To truly benefit from gratitude, we must cultivate a gratitude mindset, making it an intrinsic part of our worldview. This involves shifting from a focus on scarcity and what's missing to an appreciation for the abundance that exists in our lives. It's a transition from seeing life through a lens of comparison and discontent to one of appreciation and satisfaction.

Practices for Deepening Gratitude

Gratitude Reflection: Beyond writing in a gratitude journal, engage in regular reflection sessions where you deeply contemplate the things you're grateful for. Reflect on why these things matter to you and how they impact your life, allowing yourself to fully experience the feelings of gratitude.

Gratitude Visits: Write a letter of thanks to someone who has made a significant impact on your life and deliver it in person, if possible. This exercise not only deepens your sense of gratitude but also strengthens your relationships.

Volunteering and Acts of Kindness: Engaging in acts of kindness or volunteering for causes you care about can heighten your sense of gratitude by highlighting the positive impact you can have on others' lives. This outward expression of gratitude and compassion reinforces your internal feelings of gratitude.

The Broader Impact of Gratitude

Enhancing Emotional Well-Being: Regular practice of gratitude can significantly enhance emotional well-being by increasing positive emotions, reducing the risk of depression, and fostering resilience. It helps shift the focus from what's wrong to what's right, contributing to a more optimistic outlook on life.

Strengthening Social Bonds: Gratitude naturally fosters stronger social bonds and relationships. Expressing gratitude to others makes them feel valued and appreciated, which in turn encourages a positive social environment. These strengthened bonds contribute to a supportive community that enhances everyone's well-being.

Promoting Physical Health: Studies have shown that gratitude can have tangible benefits on physical health, including improved sleep quality, reduced symptoms of physical illness, and higher levels of physical activity. By reducing stress and promoting a positive mental state, gratitude contributes to better overall health.

Living with Gratitude and Joy

Adopting a lifestyle of gratitude and joy is a profound commitment to recognizing and appreciating the beauty in our lives, the kindness of others, and the multitude of blessings, both big and small, that we encounter daily. It's about choosing to live with a heart full of appreciation, which in turn colors our experiences, relationships, and the world around us with hues of joy and contentment.

As this chapter concludes, remember that the journey of cultivating gratitude and joy is a personal and ongoing one. It's a path paved with moments of profound realization, deep connection, and heartfelt appreciation. By choosing gratitude and joy, we choose to embrace life's full spectrum, finding richness in the ordinary and extraordinary alike, and opening ourselves to a world filled with wonder, kindness, and happiness.

Self-Reflection Questions for Personal Knowledge

1. Reflect on a challenging time in your life. Can you identify any aspect of that situation for which you can now feel grateful? How does acknowledging that aspect change your perspective on the experience?

____

____

____

____

____

2. Think about the people in your life. Who has made a significant impact on you, and have you ever expressed your gratitude to them? Consider how you might convey your appreciation and what difference it could make to both of you.

3. Evaluate your daily routine. Where can you incorporate moments of gratitude into your day? Identify specific times or triggers that could remind you to pause and acknowledge something you're grateful for.

4. Consider your physical well-being. How might a practice of gratitude positively affect your physical health? Are there any changes you notice in your body when you actively practice gratitude?

5. Assess your social interactions. How does expressing gratitude change the dynamics of your relationships? Can you recall a time when gratitude deepened a connection with someone else?

Chapter Summary

Chapter 8, "Cultivating Gratitude and Joy," delves into the profound impact that gratitude has on transforming our lives, fostering a sense of joy, and enhancing our overall well-being. The chapter opens with an exploration of the transformative power of gratitude, highlighting how this practice shifts our focus from what we lack to the abundance that surrounds us. It underscores gratitude's role in changing our perspective, allowing us to see and appreciate the value in our everyday experiences and relationships.

The discussion then moves to practical ways to cultivate gratitude and joy in our daily lives. It suggests keeping a gratitude journal, engaging in gratitude meditation, expressing gratitude to others, setting up visual reminders, and taking nature walks as simple yet effective practices. These activities are presented not just as exercises but as gateways to a more fulfilling and joyful life.

The chapter also examines the impact of gratitude on our happiness and well-being. It presents evidence from positive psychology research that shows how a gratitude practice can enhance mood, improve mental health, strengthen relationships, and even contribute to physical health. The narrative emphasizes that gratitude not only benefits the individual practitioner but also has a ripple effect, improving the social environment by fostering positive interactions and deeper connections.

In its conclusion, "Cultivating Gratitude and Joy" invites readers to integrate gratitude into their lives as a continuous practice. It encourages embracing gratitude not just as a response to positive events but as a lifestyle choice that can transform one's outlook on life. By choosing to focus on gratitude and joy, we open ourselves to a richer, more connected, and satisfying life experience, marked by an appreciation for the present moment and the myriad blessings it holds.

This chapter serves as both a practical guide and an inspirational call to action, encouraging readers to embark on a journey of gratitude and joy that enriches every aspect of their lives. Through personal reflection and the adoption of gratitude practices, we can all tap into the transformative power of gratitude, leading to a more joyful, contented, and meaningful life.

CHAPTER 9

BUILDING RESILIENCE

"Resilience is not what happens to you. It's how you react to, respond to, and recover from what happens to you." – Jeffrey Gitomer

In an ever-changing and often challenging world, resilience stands as the bedrock of emotional and mental strength, enabling us to navigate the storms of life with grace and come out stronger on the other side. Chapter 9 dives deep into the essence of building resilience, offering strategies for fortifying emotional and mental resilience, learning from failures and setbacks, and understanding the critical role of a support system in this transformative process.

Strategies for Developing Emotional and Mental Resilience

Resilience is the ability to sustain adversity and triumph over difficult life events. Building resilience is a dynamic process that involves developing certain thoughts, behaviors, and actions that can be learned over time. Here are key strategies for fostering emotional and mental resilience:

Cultivate a Positive Outlook: Maintaining a hopeful outlook is a cornerstone of resilience. This doesn't mean ignoring reality but rather choosing to focus on what you can control and find the potential for growth in challenges.

Embrace Change: Flexibility is an essential aspect of resilience. Being open to change and adaptable in the face of uncertainty can reduce the fear and anxiety that come with the unknown.

Develop Problem-Solving Skills: Resilient individuals face problems head-on, seeking solutions rather than avoiding issues. Enhancing your problem-solving skills can improve your ability to deal with life's challenges effectively.

Practice Self-Care: Taking care of your body and mind can boost your resilience. Regular exercise, adequate sleep, healthy eating, and mindfulness practices are all crucial for maintaining emotional and mental balance.

Set Realistic Goals: Break down your goals into manageable steps and take action regularly, even when faced with setbacks.

Achieving small successes can boost your confidence and motivation.

Learning from Failures and Setbacks

Failure is not the opposite of success; it's a vital part of growth and resilience building. Learning from failures involves:

Reframing Failure: View failures as opportunities to learn and grow rather than as a reflection of your worth. This mindset shift is essential for resilience.

Analyzing What Went Wrong: Take the time to understand the factors that contributed to the failure. What can be learned, and what can be done differently next time?

Fostering Grit and Perseverance: Resilience is fueled by grit—the determination to pursue your long-term goals despite difficulties. Cultivate perseverance by staying committed to your goals and viewing setbacks as temporary hurdles.

The Importance of a Support System and How to Build One

No one builds resilience in isolation. A strong support system is invaluable for providing emotional support, offering different perspectives, and encouraging you during tough times.

Nurture Your Relationships: Invest time and energy in building close relationships with family, friends, and colleagues. These bonds can offer support and encouragement when you need it most.

Seek Out Mentors: Mentors can offer guidance, advice, and a sense of stability during challenging periods. Look for individuals who have experience and wisdom to share.

Build a Community: Engage with groups or communities that share your interests or values. Whether through volunteer work, clubs, or online forums, finding a sense of belonging can bolster your resilience.

Learn to Ask for Help: Recognize when you need support and be willing to ask for it. Reaching out for help is important, it's not a sign of weakness.

Embracing the Journey of Resilience

Building resilience is a continuous process of growth and learning. It's about developing the inner strength to navigate life's ups and downs with courage and determination. This guide on your journey to resilience provides you with the tools and strategies needed to strengthen your emotional and mental fortitude, learn from life's inevitable setbacks, and create a supportive network that will stand with you through thick and thin.

By integrating these practices into your life, you can cultivate a resilient spirit that not only survives but thrives in the face of adversity, transforming challenges into opportunities for growth and self-discovery.

As we further explore the landscape of resilience, it becomes apparent that this journey is not just about surviving adversities but also about thriving amidst them. Resilience is a multifaceted trait that, once cultivated, can significantly enhance one's quality of life, fostering a sense of empowerment and well-being even in the most challenging circumstances. Let's delve deeper into additional aspects of building resilience and how they can be integrated into daily life.

Strengthening Emotional Intelligence

A key component of resilience is emotional intelligence—the ability to understand and manage your own emotions and those of the people around you. Developing emotional intelligence involves:

Self-awareness: Cultivate an understanding of your emotions, triggers, and responses. This awareness is the first step in managing your emotional reactions effectively.

Self-regulation: Learn strategies to calm yourself when you're upset. Techniques such as deep breathing, meditation, or physical exercise can help regulate your emotions and reduce stress.

Empathy: Practice seeing situations from others' perspectives. Empathy strengthens your relationships and supports a mutual support system, which is crucial for resilience.

Incorporating Mindfulness Practices

Mindfulness can significantly bolster resilience by helping you stay present and engaged, even in the face of difficulties. Mindfulness practices encourage a non-judgmental awareness of the present moment, which can help you better navigate stress, reduce rumination, and avoid being overwhelmed by negative emotions.

Daily Mindfulness Meditation: Even a few minutes of meditation each day can improve your focus, reduce stress, and enhance emotional regulation.

Mindful Walking: Turn regular walks into mindfulness exercises by focusing on the sensation of walking and the environment around you, fostering a sense of calm and presence.

Building Physical Resilience

Physical resilience is closely linked to emotional and mental resilience. A healthy body can support a healthy mind, providing you with the energy and strength needed to cope with stress and bounce back from adversity.

Regular Exercise: Physical activity not only strengthens your body but also releases endorphins, chemicals in your brain that act as natural painkillers and mood elevators.

Nutritious Diet: Eating a balanced diet provides the necessary nutrients for your body and brain to function optimally, enhancing your ability to manage stress.

Adequate Rest: Ensure you get enough sleep each night. Sleep is crucial for emotional and mental recovery, helping you process and cope with the day's events.

The Power of Perspective

Finally, building resilience often involves a shift in perspective. How you perceive and interpret the events of your life can dramatically influence your resilience.

View Challenges as Opportunities: Try to see obstacles not as insurmountable problems but as opportunities to learn, grow, and adapt. This perspective can transform your approach to adversity.

Maintain a Hopeful Outlook: A hopeful outlook enables you to expect that good things will happen in your life. Practice visualizing what you want, rather than worrying about what you fear.

Embrace Failure as a Teacher: Remember that failure is a part of the journey to success. Each failure offers valuable lessons that can pave the way for future achievements.

Embodying Resilience

Resilience is not just a tool for survival; it's a way of living that embraces growth, change, and adversity as integral parts of the human experience. By cultivating emotional and mental resilience, learning from failures and setbacks, and building a strong support system, you equip yourself with the strength to face life's challenges with confidence and grace.

Enhancing Resilience Through Continuous Learning

The pursuit of knowledge and the continuous quest for personal development are fundamental to enhancing resilience. Every new skill learned, concept mastered, or insight gained contributes to a more robust and adaptable mindset. Continuous learning encourages cognitive flexibility, a key component of resilience that enables individuals to better manage change, solve problems creatively, and adjust to new situations with ease.

Strategies for Continuous Learning:

Set Learning Goals: specify areas of interest or skills you wish to enhance. Setting simple, achievable goals can guide your learning journey and provide a sense of accomplishment.

Embrace Curiosity: Cultivate a mindset of curiosity about the world around you. Ask questions, seek out new experiences, and explore topics outside of your comfort zone.

Learn from Diverse Sources: Expand your horizons by learning from a variety of sources—books, online courses, podcasts, workshops, and people with different perspectives and backgrounds.

Reflect on Your Learning: Take time to reflect on what you've learned and how it applies to your life. Reflection deepens understanding and reinforces learning.

Fostering a Culture of Resilience

Building resilience is not only an individual endeavor but also a communal one. Fostering a culture of resilience within families, workplaces, and communities creates an environment where people support each other in overcoming challenges, adapting to change, and thriving in the face of adversity.

Creating a Resilient Environment:

Promote Open Communication: Encourage the sharing of thoughts, feelings, and experiences. Open communication builds trust and makes it easier for individuals to seek and offer support.

Cultivate a Positive Outlook: Model and encourage optimism and a positive approach to problem-solving. A collective focus on solutions rather than problems can uplift the entire group.

Encourage Mutual Support: Build networks of support where members actively look out for one another. Sharing resources, knowledge, and encouragement strengthens communal resilience.

Recognize and Celebrate Resilience: Acknowledge acts of resilience within the community. Celebrating these achievements reinforces the value of resilience and inspires others.

Personal Stories of Resilience

Personal stories of resilience serve as powerful testimonies to the human spirit's ability to overcome adversity. These narratives often share common themes of enduring hardship, discovering inner strength, and emerging transformed. Let's explore a few examples that illustrate the diverse ways individuals exhibit resilience.

Example 1: Malala Yousafzai - Advocacy in the Face of Adversity

Malala Yousafzai's story is one of remarkable resilience and courage. As a young girl in Pakistan, Malala advocated for girls' education, despite the Taliban's threats and eventual violent attack on her life. Her resilience in the face of such danger, her recovery from a life-threatening injury, and her unwavering commitment to her cause have inspired millions. Malala's journey from a targeted activist to the youngest Nobel Prize laureate highlights the power of resilience rooted in conviction and the pursuit of justice.

Example 2: Viktor Frankl - Finding Meaning in Suffering

Viktor Frankl, a neurologist, psychiatrist, and Holocaust survivor offers a profound example of resilience through his experience in Nazi concentration camps. In his book, "Man's Search for Meaning," Frankl describes how finding personal meaning in the most harrowing of circumstances, including immense suffering and loss, can provide the strength to endure. His development of logotherapy, a form of psychotherapy that emphasizes the search for life's meaning, underscores resilience as a journey of discovering purpose in the face of adversity.

Example 3: Stephen Hawking - Overcoming Physical Limitations

Stephen Hawking's resilience in the face of amyotrophic lateral sclerosis (ALS) is a testament to the human ability to adapt and thrive despite physical limitations. Diagnosed with a motor neuron disease at 21 and given just a few years to live, Hawking defied expectations by making groundbreaking contributions to cosmology and theoretical physics. His determination to pursue his work, despite the progression of his illness, and his efforts to communicate complex scientific ideas to the public, demonstrate resilience through intellectual pursuit and innovation.

Example 4: Oprah Winfrey - Triumph Over Early Life Challenges

Oprah Winfrey's rise from poverty, abuse, and discrimination to become one of the most influential media personalities and philanthropists in the world is a powerful story of resilience. Oprah's ability to transform her painful early experiences into a force for positive change, empathy, and empowerment for others showcases how resilience can be a catalyst for transformation and advocacy.

Example 5: Elizabeth Smart - Healing and Activism After Trauma

Elizabeth Smart's abduction at 14 and her subsequent nine-month ordeal of captivity and abuse is a harrowing tale of survival. Her resilience is evident in her recovery and decision to become an advocate for missing persons and victims of sexual assault. Elizabeth's work in raising awareness, promoting change in laws related to child abduction and recovery, and her message of hope and healing to other survivors underscores the potential for resilience to foster advocacy and support for others facing similar challenges.

These stories illustrate that resilience can manifest in various forms, whether through advocacy, finding meaning in suffering, overcoming physical limitations, transforming personal trauma into empowerment, or intellectual pursuit. Each narrative provides unique insights into the journey of resilience, showing that while the nature of adversity may differ, the core of resilience lies in the human capacity to endure, adapt, and find strength in the struggle.

Learning from Resilience Stories:

Identify with the Journey: Look for elements of the story that resonate with your own experiences. Identifying with the storyteller can provide comfort and a sense of shared humanity.

Extract the Lessons: Pay attention to the strategies and mindsets that helped the individuals overcome their challenges. Consider how these lessons can be applied to your own life.

Share Your Own Story: If you feel comfortable, share your own story of resilience. Your narrative could be the beacon of hope someone else needs.

Self-Reflection Questions for Personal Knowledge

1. Reflect on a time in your life when you faced significant adversity. What strengths did you discover in yourself during that time, and how did the experience shape your understanding of resilience?

____

____

____

____

____

2. Think about a story of resilience that particularly inspires you. What aspects of this story resonate most with you, and how can you apply the lessons learned from this story to your own life?

____

____

____

____

____

3. Consider the role of support systems in your journey of resilience. Who has been a part of your support system during difficult times, and how have they helped you navigate challenges?

____

____

____

____

____

4. Recall a failure or setback that you initially struggled with. How did you eventually overcome or learn from this experience, and what does that teach you about your capacity for resilience?

____

____

____

____

____

5. Identify a situation where you demonstrated resilience without initially recognizing it. Looking back, how do you

view this experience differently now, and what does it reveal about your ability to adapt and persevere?

Chapter Summary

Chapter 9, "Building Resilience," delves into the concept of resilience as an essential quality that enables individuals to navigate life's challenges with strength and grace. The chapter begins by outlining strategies for developing emotional and mental resilience, emphasizing the importance of maintaining a positive outlook, embracing change, enhancing problem-solving skills, practicing self-care, and setting realistic goals.

We then explore the crucial process of learning from failures and setbacks. This section highlights the value of reframing failure as a learning opportunity, analyzing mistakes to foster growth, and cultivating grit and perseverance. By embracing these approaches, individuals can transform their experiences of failure into stepping stones for success. The chapter also addresses the importance of building and maintaining a robust support system. It offers guidance on nurturing relationships, seeking out mentors, engaging with supportive communities, and learning to ask for help when needed. This support network is presented as a foundational element of resilience, providing emotional backing, advice, and encouragement.

Personal stories of resilience, including those of notable figures such as Malala Yousafzai, Viktor Frankl, Stephen Hawking, Oprah Winfrey, and Elizabeth Smart, are woven throughout the chapter to illustrate the diverse manifestations of resilience. These narratives showcase the power of resilience in overcoming adversity, finding meaning in suffering, overcoming physical and mental limitations, and transforming personal trauma into advocacy and empowerment.

"Building Resilience" serves as both a practical guide and a source of inspiration for individuals seeking to strengthen their resilience. Through a combination of strategic practices, a mindset geared toward growth and learning, and the support of a compassionate community, readers are encouraged to cultivate resilience as a way of life. This journey of building resilience is portrayed as an ongoing process, one that enriches individuals' capacity to face life's challenges with courage, adaptability, and an unwavering spirit of perseverance.

CHAPTER 10

LIVING AUTHENTICALLY

"To thine own self be true, and it must follow, as the night the day, thou canst not then be false to any man." – William Shakespeare

In a world that often values conformity and the outward appearance of success, living authentically—aligned with one's values and purpose—becomes a revolutionary act. Chapter 10, "Living Authentically," explores the essence of authenticity, and its profound impact on lasting happiness, and provides practical steps for aligning your life with your true self, culminating in a personal action plan for ongoing growth and happiness.

Defining and Living According to Your Values and Purpose

Authentic living begins with a deep understanding of your values and purpose—the core principles and motivations that guide your decisions, actions, and way of being in the world. Living authentically means that your life reflects these values and purpose, even when doing so challenges societal expectations or personal comfort.

Identify Your Core Values: Reflect on what truly matters to you. What principles do you hold dear? Honesty, freedom, compassion, creativity? Identifying your core values is the first step toward living a life aligned with them.

Discover Your Purpose: Your purpose is your reason for being, your answer to the question, "Why do I get up in the morning?" It can be related to your career, but it also encompasses broader aspirations related to personal growth, relationships, and contribution to the world.

Evaluate Your Life Alignment: Assess how well your current lifestyle, career, and relationships reflect your values and purpose. Where do you see discrepancies? Acknowledging these areas is crucial for moving toward a more authentic life.

The Role of Authenticity in Lasting Happiness

Authenticity is intimately linked to lasting happiness. When you live in alignment with your true self, you experience a sense of congruence and integrity that is deeply satisfying. Conversely, living inauthentically—out of sync with your values and purpose—

can lead to feelings of disconnection, dissatisfaction, and even despair.

Authenticity Breeds Connection: Being genuine allows you to form deeper, more meaningful relationships. People are drawn to authenticity and are more likely to respond with openness and sincerity when you present your true self.

Self-Acceptance: Authentic living requires accepting all parts of yourself, including your weaknesses and imperfections. This self-acceptance is liberating and forms the foundation of genuine happiness.

Practical Steps to Align Your Life with Your True Self

Living authentically is an ongoing journey. Here are practical steps to bring your life into closer alignment with your true self:

Set Authentic Goals: Create goals that reflect your values and purpose, rather than societal expectations or external pressures. Ensure your goals are in alignment with what truly matters to you.

Practice Mindfulness and Self-Reflection: Regularly engage in mindfulness and self-reflection to stay connected with your inner self. This practice helps you remain aware of your values and purpose and notice when you're drifting from them.

Cultivate Courage: Living authentically often requires courage to stand up for your beliefs and make choices that may not be popular or easy. Recognize that the fulfillment and happiness that come from authenticity are worth these challenges.

Seek Supportive Environments and Relationships: Surround yourself with people and environments that support your authentic self. A supportive community can encourage you to express your true self and pursue your genuine aspirations.

Creating a Personal Action Plan for Ongoing Growth and Happiness

A personal action plan is a dynamic tool for guiding your journey to authenticity. It involves setting specific, actionable steps to align your life with your values and purpose. Include short-term and long-term goals, strategies for overcoming obstacles, and methods for tracking your progress.

Review and Adjust Regularly: Your values, purpose, and understanding of your authentic self may evolve. Regularly review and adjust your action plan to reflect your current understanding and aspirations.

Celebrate Your Progress: Embrace and celebrate your achievements along the line. Recognizing your progress reinforces your commitment to living authentically and motivates continued growth.

Self-Reflection Questions for Personal Knowledge

1. What are three core values that resonate deeply with you? Reflect on how these values currently manifest in your life. Are there areas where you feel you're not fully living in alignment with these values?

____

____

____

____

____

2. Can you articulate your purpose or a sense of mission that drives you? How does this purpose influence your daily actions and long-term goals? If you find it difficult to define, consider what activities or pursuits make you feel most alive and fulfilled.

____

____

____

____

____

3. Recall a moment when you felt you had to mask your true self to fit in or please others. How did this affect your sense of well-being and happiness? What would it have taken to remain authentic in that situation?

____

____

____

____

____

4. What goals have you pursued because you felt you 'should,' based on external expectations or societal norms? How do these goals differ from those you would choose based on your authentic self?

____

____

____

____

5. Identify one step you can take this week to live more authentically. This could be a small action aligned with your core values, speaking your truth in a situation where you might normally remain silent, or dedicating time to a passion that genuinely reflects who you are.

____

____

____

____

Chapter Summary

Chapter 10, "Living Authentically," explores the profound journey of aligning one's life with their true values, purpose, and essence. It begins with defining authenticity as the practice of understanding, accepting, and expressing one's true self, highlighting its crucial role in achieving lasting happiness and fulfillment. The chapter underscores the importance of living by one's values and purpose, pointing out that authenticity is not just about being true to oneself but also about creating a life that reflects that truth in every aspect.

Strategies for living authentically are then detailed, starting with the identification of core values and a sense of purpose. It emphasizes the need for self-reflection and mindfulness as tools for maintaining a connection with one's authentic self, and the courage required to make choices that align with one's true values, even when faced with opposition or misunderstanding.

The role of authenticity in fostering lasting happiness is thoroughly examined, showing how genuine living leads to deeper connections with others, increased self-acceptance, and a more fulfilling life. Practical steps for aligning life with one's true self include setting authentic goals, practicing mindfulness, cultivating the courage to live by one's values, and seeking supportive environments that encourage authenticity.

The chapter concludes with guidance on creating a personal action plan for ongoing growth and happiness. This plan involves setting specific, actionable steps to ensure that one's daily actions and long-term goals reflect their authentic self. It encourages regular review and adjustment of the plan to accommodate personal growth and changing understandings of authenticity.

"Living Authentically" serves as a comprehensive guide for anyone seeking to embrace their true self and live a life of genuine fulfillment. It provides readers with the tools and insights needed to embark on a journey of self-discovery, resilience, and profound personal transformation, highlighting that the path to true happiness and satisfaction lies in authenticity.

CONCLUSION

Beyond the Illusion

"The greatest discovery of any generation is that a human can alter his life by altering his attitude." – William James

As we draw the curtains on this transformative journey, it's essential to reflect on the profound insights and lessons that have emerged from "Beyond the Illusion." This concluding chapter is not merely an end but a new beginning, offering a synthesis of key learnings, practical advice for integrating these lessons into daily life, and encouragement for the ongoing journey toward a life of genuine happiness and fulfillment.

Summarizing Key Insights and Lessons from the Journey

This journey began with an exploration of the happiness trap, the realization that chasing after fleeting pleasures or societal measures of success often leads us away from true fulfillment. Through each chapter, we've uncovered layers of wisdom on cultivating self-awareness, embracing vulnerability, building resilience, living authentically, and finding joy in gratitude. These are not just chapters in a book but chapters in the story of our lives, each offering valuable insights:

Self-Awareness: The foundation of personal growth, providing the clarity needed to navigate life's challenges and opportunities.

Vulnerability: A strength that fosters genuine connections and allows us to face our fears with courage.

Resilience: The ability to bounce back from adversity, learning from our experiences to emerge stronger.

Authenticity: Living in alignment with our true values and purpose, the cornerstone of lasting happiness.

Gratitude: A transformative practice that shifts our focus from what we lack to the abundance that surrounds us.

Integrating the Book's Lessons into Daily Life

To bring these insights into the fabric of our daily lives, we must approach each day as an opportunity to practice these principles. This means:

Making Mindful Choices: Pause to consider whether your actions align with your values and contribute to your well-being.

Embracing Challenges as Opportunities: View setbacks as chances to grow, asking what can be learned rather than why it happened.

Cultivating a Gratitude Practice: Start or end each day by reflecting on three things you are grateful for, no matter how small.

Seeking Connection: Reach out to others with openness and empathy, building relationships that nurture your authentic self.

Encouragement for the Journey Ahead

As you move forward, remember that personal growth is a continuous journey of learning and adaptation. Life will inevitably present new challenges, but each obstacle is also an opportunity to apply these lessons, deepen your understanding, and refine your approach to living a fulfilled life.

Stay Curious: Keep an open mind and a willing heart. Curiosity fuels growth and keeps the journey interesting.

Be Patient with Yourself: Change takes time. Celebrate your progress, no matter how small, and be compassionate with yourself through the ups and downs.

Remain Committed to Your Growth: Revisit these lessons often, adapt them to new circumstances, and stay committed to your path of personal development.

Final Thoughts on Living a Life Filled with Genuine Happiness and Fulfillment

Living a life filled with genuine happiness and fulfillment is possible when we move beyond the illusion—beyond the external markers of success and fleeting pleasures—to embrace the in-depth truths of who we are and what matters to us. This book has been a guide on that journey, providing tools and insights to help you uncover your authentic self, build resilience, and cultivate a life of joy and meaning.

Remember, the path to fulfillment is not a destination but a manner of traveling. It's about the choices we make each day, the attitudes we adopt, and the openness with which we embrace life's ever-unfolding journey. As you continue on your path, carry these lessons with you, let them guide your steps, and trust that you have everything within you to create a life of deep satisfaction and joy.

"Escaping the Illusion of Happiness" has been your companion on this journey, but the next chapters are yours to write, with the pen of your actions, the ink of your experiences, and the paper of your daily life. Here's to living a life that resonates with the truth of who you are, filled with the joy of being authentically you.

NOTES

THANK YOU FOR READING THIS BOOK

Dear Esteemed Readers,

From the depths of my heart, I extend my sincerest gratitude for joining me on the profound journey that "Escaping the Illusion of Happiness" has offered. Your unwavering commitment to exploring the landscapes of self-awareness, resilience, and authenticity has illuminated the path for this book's creation. Your dedication to personal growth and transformation is a beacon that has shaped every word and insight within these pages.

Should you find yourself with questions or in need of further clarity regarding any aspect of this journey, please do not hesitate to reach out to me at [speaktolivia@gmail.com]. Your thoughts, experiences, and feedback are not only welcomed but invaluable as they contribute to the ongoing dialogue of living authentically and fully.

I hope that "Escaping the Illusion of Happiness" has been a source of inspiration and guidance for you.

If you could spare a moment to share your honest feedback on this book, it would be immensely appreciated. Your insights can help extend the reach of this message, enabling more individuals to navigate their path to genuine happiness and fulfillment.

With warmest regards and gratitude for your journey,
Olivia Tranquil